Dandelions Don't Cry

Sowmini S K

BookLeaf Publishing

India | USA | UK

Made with ❤ on the BookLeaf Publishing Platform
www.bookleafpub.in
www.bookleafpub.com

Dedication

For the green bird that visits me every day

Acknowledgement

I am grateful to my family, friends, professors, and all others who inspired me to break out of my shell and discover the world through the power of words. Also, thanks to the myriad experiences of life that have shaped me, my beliefs, and my writings.

Preface

In the quiet moments between dawn and dusk, where the world seems to hold its breath, poetry finds its voice. *Dandelions Don't Cry* is an invitation to explore these fleeting pauses in life, captured through verse. This collection seeks to illuminate the ordinary, celebrating the simple joys and profound sorrows that shape our existence. Each poem is a reflection, a fragment of a larger mosaic that captures the essence of our shared humanity. As you read, I hope you find echoes of your own experiences and emotions, and that these verses offer solace and a sense of connection. Welcome to a journey through the poetic landscape of existence.

Table of Contents

1. An Ode to My Pillow

My pillow, my companion,
through years of slumber and rest,
holding me close and tight,
in the darkness and din of the night;
Together, we've seen a million dreams,
in shades of snow white and grey;
wandering across mountains and streams,
to mystic lands, far away.

You smiled in a kindly light,
when I chuckled loud and clear,
amidst heaves and snores,
in the saintly silence of the night.
You wrapped me in a warm embrace,
when my eyes wet your bosom,
amidst sniffs and stifled cries,
in the sullen glow of the night.

You gave me hope for a better day,
as I tossed around helplessly,
with no sign of sleep or peace,
like a boat in a stormy bay.
You cradled me in your arms,
when I woke up, aghast,
shaken by hideous dreams,
from the shadows of the past.

You've known my smiles and sorrows,
my deeper scents and strains;
You are my beacon and armor,
as I wade through a sea of pains.
I cherish this mystic bond we share;
in a world of deceit and dare,
my pillow, my friend,
you nourish my soul with the nectar of love and
care.

2. You won't understand

why I stand at the doorway every night with
bated
breath, a gleam in my eyes, eager to pour out the
tidings of the day — a broken pencil, a pulled
ponytail,
a lost water bottle, forgotten homework, a
half-eaten
sandwich, a stray puppy, a tug of war in the bus,
a missed catch that broke Ramu Kaka's window.
the frogs
in the marsh croak anxiously — ribbit-ribbit; I
cover my
ears with my palms, blocking out all noise except
the pounding of my heart. ribbit-ribbit slips
through the space between my fingers and flows
into the dark abyss of my ears.
ribbit-ribbit-ribbit-ribbit.
the cries reach a
crescendo as the first drops
of rain descend upon the Earth
and your footsteps enter the gate.

how my face withers when you walk past me and
the frogs, deep into the house, shedding a slight
smile, a minuscule one like the *jeeraga mittai*

you thrust in my mouth when I bellow
at the tea shop, the bus stop, or
the village fair.
Small, sweet, and confusing. A whiff of cologne
I catch as you pass by.
The frogs raise their ugly heads and croak,
drenched in the scent of the rain.
ribbit-ribbit. You eat dinner; I watch in silence.
You wash your hands; I wipe my tears.
You rest your head on the plush pillow; I
hold my head in
my hands. You snore as loud as the silence
echoing within me. You babble
in deep sleep, incoherent words, incomplete
sentences;
the blanks are never
filled; I stand staring at the void, waiting for you
to go out again and return.
ribbit-ribbit.

3. The Little One

Little raindrops adorn your face
Eyeing me quietly with a puzzled gaze.
Pink roses blossom bright,
On your dimples, lovely and light.

Gentle folds of skin, so smooth
Like silken weaves of fine fabric;
Faint and feathery to the touch,
Lacing my heart with heavenly magic.

Petite fingers trap my tresses; tiny,
Tangled tendrils stuck to your palms,
You relish these curls of black,
Like buzzing bees on a flowery stack.

Sometimes a coo, sometimes a gurgle —
The symphony you make all day;
No mortal or soaring bird
Has sung a more mellifluous warble.

The scent of a million roses, I feel
The fragrance of innocence, whole
As I embrace you, my little bundle
In the swaddle of my soul.

A ray of sunshine in my arms,
A slice of the moon on a starry night,
Boundless bliss and harmony,
I wish you in your life's journey.

4. Once upon a time

Once upon a time, in distant Konkan
Was a sleepy hamlet, still and sunken
Over a valley, scenic and serene,
Laden with myths and mysteries, unseen.

The day they found her, cold and blue
By the banks of the silver stream,
Rumors rolled down the roads,
Terrible tales imagined, some true.

"Who is she?" queried the police.
"Shyama," answered the crowd.
"Her husband?" he inquired.
"All of us," giggled the men around.

Like cacti on desert sands,
Like algae on still ponds,
She thrived on her own,
Told the villagers with a frown.

Clues collected with fervor;
Suspects studied with rigor;
Evidence examined with heed;
But none to deplore the deed.

Canines sniffed around her body,
Like those random men at night,
Intoxicated with local toddy,
Drowning in her dark, heavy scent.

"Who did it?" wondered the mob.
Shyama was brave, headstrong;
No mortal uttered a sigh nor a sob;
"Suits her!" whispered the throng.

A pair of eyes in the crowd stared
As they wrapped her in a white robe;
His face went pale, his nostrils flared;
Sweat trickled down his left earlobe.

The police left the place, sulking
Weary of the routine, long and taxing.
The mob scattered into slender lanes,
Past fields of corn and sugarcanes.

Reports arrived a month later.
"Suicide!" proclaimed every paper.
"She had consumed poison," they said
And slyly buried all news of the dead.

A pair of eyes in the village still wept;
Shyama's memories and secrets he kept.
The lone son of the chieftain, revered;
Her sweet scent in his heart, he treasured.

His hands stroked her tresses as she slept,
Like a child close to his bosom. He wept
With this illusion tormenting him all night,
Clandestine, he hid the poison from sight.

They found him in the well one day,
Rotten with remorse and grief;
His body still, his heart throbbing
With love, he concealed like a thief.

A dark red ribbon on his wrist swayed;
The curly hair on his chest prayed
To be one with her, blending bold
With her scent in the other world.

5. Winter Rain

Flowers in the winter rain
murmur through the winds of might,
unknown to the turf below,
Fables of strife and strain.

Drooping their heads so low,
brooding over bygone days
of sunlight and chirpy birds,
they tremble in fright and woe.

Crickets and bees alike,
tangoed on petals so bright,
daintily in dreamy land,
distant from this icy night.

The soft tint of a butterfly,
the warm touch of a golden sun,
embraced the little blossoms,
on days of the summer sky.

Stroking their heads, so light
whispered the gentle breeze,
"I have to leave tonight,
before the mountains freeze."

The roaring skies took away
their only friend, so dear
as the little petals cried,
lost in a land so wide.

Chilly nights rolled by
buried in snow and pain;
longing for a lullaby,
the blooms curl and fade away.

The broken wing of a tiny bug
falls on a buttercup, stirring
the frozen heart and painting
hopes of a sprightly sky.

The petite petals raise their heads,
from mounds of snowy beds;
Gazing at the passing clouds,
They dream of a saintly glow.

6. The Snail

A snail arrived at my garden today, slow and
steady.
he is spectacular; reminds me

of the little kid next door sauntering to school
reluctantly,
in half-draped uniform clothes, an untied
shoelace,
braving the fury of yelling parents and fiery of
the yellowing sun;

of the Alleppey fish curry simmering in the
earthen pot,
infused with kokum, blended with coconut,
seasoned
with spices, laced with curry leaves, slow-cooked
to Godly perfection, made only on special days
for special guests, ones from the upper league,
the less privileged
bestowed with leftovers, a gift for their saintly
patience;

of the tiny creek by my house, flowing quietly,
unperturbed,

not intruding into the penance of the passersby,
drinking in
the stillness of life and the unequivocal flow of
the current;

of the fast and futile life I am leading, leading me
to nowhere. caught in a mad rush to conquer
lengths and
breadths and heights, existent only in lands
conjured by
figments, frail and imaginary; the fear of missing
out, of
fitting in, of standing out, of falling, of falling
apart, of
failing, of fleeing, terrible fears of every form,
shape and
kind, looming large and wild; creeping in the
night, scary
strangling my breath, dreary;

Never a respite from this struggle, ominous and
omniscient.
a lifetime of crawling, walking, sleepwalking,
sprinting, racing,
bruised and burnt; crawling again; a journey
unfulfilled, towards the unkind unknown.

the snail is receding into his shell; he is
spectacular; he reminds me
of the living lords, less extraordinary, clutching
their seats
tight, in cabins and cabinets, sabhas and samitis,
sevas and sangams, on soil and the seas,
showing me my own
space, safe and secluded; my solace; the bubble to
which I belong; the cocoon I call home;
home alone, far from
the madding crowd, away from the crowding
cries, sheltered from
the roaring skies, licking my wounds,
nursing my soul, singing
to myself, lullabies and laments for those I hold
dear; for the
sinned and sinful, the born and the dead, gone
with the wind.

7. A Note to an Introvert

In the meeting, I see you —
a dot in the darkness,
a drop in the ocean,
a speck of dust in the universe;
nodding,
smiling,
listening
till the last word is spoken.

At the social, I see you -
a startled snail,
a lost lamb,
a shrinking violet;
blinking,
fiddling,
sinking
into the silence within you.

In your room, I see you —
deep in thought,
submerged in solitude,
brimming with ideas;
writing,
reading,
singing

blissfully in your solo world.

Every dawn, I see you — the invisible
whispering to the winds,
wielding your wand,
weaving little magic,
crisply,
quietly,
deeply,
from the stillness of your shell.

8. The Green Bird

Every morning, as the day breaks
And the silver dews sparkle bright,
Arrives a green bird at my window;
A little one, dainty and daring.

She taps with her beak, so gently
And hums a mellifluous strain;
Pretty plumes spread in delight,
Filling my soul with a quaint light.

I walk in stealth towards her, beaming
She flaps her wings with grace and glee.
With wondrous flair and finesse,
She descends on a distant tree.

My feathered friend, tranquil and dear
Drowns my memories of the night
As she sings in a voice so clear
Ushering in peace and respite.

Her notes, so plaintive and calm
Carries me to an age of yore
Sans sins and sorrows, basking
In bliss never felt before.

Upon me, she has cast a divine spell
Which I wish never to quell.
Oh, little bird! I await your birth
On my heart's sanctum, today and evermore.

9. Lost Love

Slowly & softly rolled the tears
Down the frills of her gentle cheeks
Stressed & submerged in unknown fears
Sleep had deserted her eyes since bygone weeks.

Her head quivered every passing second;
Buried in the fathoms of the pillow, moist &
sullen
No hand to caress, no soul to depend
On, she drifted deep into her world of pathos &
burden.

Fond memories of childhood, misty & green
Rose before her like imposing shadows in the
gloomy night
Many a butterfly, many a daffodil had she seen
Past gleeful lanes of golden summer & spring
bright.

That mystique August evening, amidst kith & kin
When heavens watched & angels whispered
wishes with a wand
Feathery dreams took flight, lost in the clouds,
lost in the din

The loving hearts walked down the aisle, both
hand in hand.

Years fled silently in peace & gay abandon
As their children grew entwined in a bond of
blissful harmony
Life swept them to faraway shores, with prizes
laden
She thrived on lonely lands meekly, with little
love and no money.

The skies wept & the storm roared with furious
might
When they brought home his body, cold & blue
on a lifeless bed
A faint gleam shone; a dead leaf stirred that
frosty night
When her heart bled, life choked & an ocean of
salty tears she shed.

Little had time erased the memories of seasoned
woes
Which she bore with fear & agony, close to her
bosom
Through the window, a stream of stealthy air
touched her toes
As she lay on the dusty floors of the old age
home.

10. In Memory

Of the breeze that brushed your hair;
the sparkle in your eyes, so fair;

Of the quiet evenings by the river;
the hands we held together;

Of the candy, I licked off your fingers;
the aftertaste that still lingers;

Of the candle that burnt during supper;
the steaming desire that took us upper;

Of the pounding hearts at the altar;
the pastor's smile that did not falter;

Of the petrichor that filled my heart;
rains that blessed a new start;

Of the red strawberries we picked,
the fond memories we clicked;

Of the first burst of anger you expressed,
the trickle of tears I suppressed;

Of the silence that filled our room;

the night I awaited you in gloom;

Of the frown on your face when I questioned;
your tone and eyes darkened;

Of the way your lips parted to disagree;
sheer disdain to my plea;

Of your nails that dug into my flesh;
a spider trapped in its own mesh;

Of the simmering fights, day and night;
imprints on my face, a common sight;

Of the distance that crept between us;
the maid who watched in distress;

Of all the lies we told each other,
the emptiness that stayed forever;

Of the storm that raged in and out;
the pain that struck me like a clout;

Of that Sunday I made your favorite curry;
spices and magic, I mixed in a hurry;

Of the way I stopped mid-sentence;
your head wobbling in deep turbulence;

Of the blood that oozed down your pointed
nose;
the bed that held your frail body, a wilted rose;

Of the owls that watch you through the night;
the daisies dancing beside your grave, pretty
bright.

11. Stage Fright

Tremor in my knees,
A quiver on my lips,
Frozen all over,
I stand on stage, the first time ever.

A quick gaze around,
A shiver down my spine,
A glare from the boss,
I stand on stage, breathing like a horse.

A heart full of fear,
Eyes fighting a tear,
Head bent down,
I stand on stage, fiddling with the gown.

A stutter in my speech,
Struggle with my poise,
Sweat on my brow,
I stand on stage, ruining the show.

Missing many a line,
Dropping the mic down,
Nothing more to say,
I stand on stage, eager to run away.

Panic in my mind,
A murmur in the crowd,
A rushed note of thanks;
I leave the stage, never to come again.

12. The Journey

Through grey hills and green jungles,
I set forth on a journey, long and winding
Across sleepy trails and sloppy terrains
Unraveling mysteries, bleak and blinding.

The golden sun and the silver moon,
Testaments to my travels, daring
Beyond perimeters of land and water,
Kindle me with a light, kind and caring.

Purple blossoms and placid humans
I greet, at every passing turn and transit
Fears so mighty, pains so fierce
I conquer with a tactful gambit

Pearly white peaks and palm-clad beaches
Soothe my mind, restless and raging.
The sands of the Sahara and freezing Tundra
Have set ablaze a passion, soaring.

A dream so dreary, destination unknown,
Through the winding wheels of time.
Yet my love for this voyage, incessant
An undying ember in my life, sublime.

13. Knotted

Your lips are salty,
sipping droplets of tears,
incessantly flowing from
a black and white ocean.

Your eyes are swollen,
big, round, and black — your kajal
smudged, like abstract art
on a pale, passive canvas.

Your ears bleed, hearing
women, men, and priests
chant "Rest in peace"
to the non-existent.

Your chest aches heavily
with all the beating, now
letting out hidden pains
through heaves and sighs.

Your bladder hurts,
overwhelmed with fluid,
bottled up like the grief
crushing your heart.

Your head is down, bent
like a question mark, staring
at your past laid on the floor,
clothed in shades of grey.

Your mouth is open, beginning
to utter something, closes
midway, words unspoken
floating in the air.

Your fingers are numb, picking
at the end of your saree,
knotted intricately quite
like the life ahead of you.

14. Those Lines

I wake up startled as it beeps — the
monitor near the bed, with incessant
waves on it, some sinusoidal, some
flat, oft oblique; the vivid display,
the only ray of light in the room. I see
squiggly, little patterns on the screen
emerging like a steady stream, reminiscent
of the doodles in the dull white pages
of her notebook, irresistibly cute;
quirky riddles staring at me.

My heart beats in tune, resonating with
these patterns, worrying and calming
alternately. The only sound in the room
is that of her breathing; so musical, I
reflect. She plays drums at school; I see
her rhythm on the screen.

A pair of lines is all it takes. Life is first
seen as two pink lines on a strip; the end
is portrayed by a solid line on the screen;
thin lines that oscillate between hope and
despair. "The report will take a week; it's
a complicated scan," says the radiologist. "So
is my life," I mumble as I walk out of the
clinic, a lattice of lines running all over me.

15. Revenge

Flames of fury burning bright
In the chambers of my inner eye
Every passing day and night,
Eager to broil you alive!

Scores of sins and blemishes
Color your soul, black and evil
No pardon, no shelter on earth
Can save you from endless peril!

You tore apart my wings,
You stole away my dreams, solitaire
I lie aghast in an inferno
Lone, lifeless, and bare.

The spasms under your breath,
The contours crossed by your touch,
Raging, rancid reminders of such
Seething sores tearing my heart!

My hair so earl, eyes so pale
Through the turn of time and tide,
Yet, unceasing is my hunt for you
On the lanes of destiny, far and wide.

I seek revenge, cold and brutal,
Upon you — coarse, conniving mortal!
Decay in every bone and pain in every pore,
Vile, vicious torment, and nothing more.

16. Dandelions don't cry

I look outside my window
m u s i n g,
b r o o d i n g,
yearning,
memories of summers
in the valley, covered with
meadows
moist
and mushrooms
under the trees, untended,
a childhood growing wild,
under the stars
blinking,
twinkling,
running past
narrow, muddy lanes,
chasing
a million dragonflies
on warm river banks.
I wish never to be
a dragonfly,
caught
by the boys,
caged
in claustrophobic

matchboxes;
wounds in place of wings.

A bouquet
of dandelions
pale white,
f l u f f y
swaying in the b r e e z e;
Mild, miniature
p u f f balls
waltzing with the wind,
detached,
dancing,
a w a i t i n g
to be blown
away
by a stroke of breeze,
a gush of air;
petite mouths
full of
innocence.
I wish to be
a
f l y i n g
fragment
of a dandelion,
a wisp,
a whisper,

romancing the a i r;
I wish to be

a

f l o a t i n g

floret

of a dandelion,

s e r e n e

s o o t h i n g

s o f t

cotton candies

in the sky;
I wish to be

a

daring

ball

of a dandelion,

hardy,

shiny,

BOLD,

for

dandelions don't break;
dandelions don't cry.

17. Ocean Child

Incessant waves rising from the hollows
of the ocean, high and mighty,
surrender to the shores with stifled cries,
like a newborn soothed by the scent of his
mother.

The silence of the shimmering sands,
echoes past corals and crabs,
stroking their pearly white heads
and hushes the murmurs of their heaving heart.

A dazzling light from the far east,
awakens the tiny tides from a deep slumber
with an embrace so warm and golden,
ushering in the promise of a beautiful day.

Opening their big blue eyes wide,
trembling in fear of the unknown kind,
the little waves look around for faces —
Gentle, familiar, and fond.

They play all day with toys, resplendent
strewn by carefree travelers along the shore;
some benign, a few so pernicious,
silent killers masquerading as playthings.

A siesta at noon, rocked by palms in tune
with the whispers of the wind, sheltered
by floating parachutes and sturdy catamarans,
oblivious of the ebbs and flows around.

Wrapped in the misty light of the moon,
the infant waves nestle, tiny thumbs tucked
in their mouths, little snuffles in sleep,
lost in dreams of bluish-green hues.

18. I wish I were

a stray leaf floating in the air,
a speck of dust on a crowded street,
a silhouette in the summer sky,
the shadow of a passing cloud,
a tassel at the end of your saree,
a fallen eyelash that you send away with a wish.

But, alas, I am a mere mortal with
a dream in my mind, rosy
desire in my heart, red
avarice clouding my eyes, yellow
blood on my hands, scarlet.
I wash, wash, wash
rub, rub, rub.
The stains don't fade, not
from my hands, not from my heart.
I wash, wash, wash
rub, rub, rub,
in vain.
I run so f a r
away
from you,
from me,
from life,
from the dead.

Oh no!
It's a dead-end.

Nowhere to go,
I look up at the sky.
Pregnant clouds stare back,
threatening to burst at any time.

19. Metamorphosis

A blank sheet of paper;
Words trickle in
drop
by
drop
red ink from
a bruised heart.

A barren stretch of sand;
Water oozes out
thorn
by
thorn
from a broken
stem of a cactus.

Emptiness in the heart;
Hope creeps in
ray
by
ray
from the sunken
shadows of the past.

A flower blooms alone,

petal
by
petal
in the darkness
of the night, a secret unfolds.

A worm crawls on the leaf,
little
by
little
It slows down, shrinks, dies —
A butterfly is born.

A timid snail awakens;
step
by
step
It emerges from the cocoon.

A sturdy hand peels away
layer
by
layer
the inner scars; the soul is set free.

20. How Madness Begins

A silent family.
A lone child.
Closed walls.
Conversations with toys.
Mistakes made.
Eyebrows raised.
Hands raised.
Scars made.
Crumbled heart.
Stifled wails.
Omitted embrace.
Compensatory gifts.
Busy lives.
Faded smiles.

Friends found.
Words spoken.
Games played.
Dreams woven.
News arrived.

Decisions made.
Bags packed.
Homes moved.
Uprooted.

Replanted.
Wilted.
Withered.

Scary nights.
Spiteful years.
Low self-esteem.
Lonely life.
Agnostic.
Antisocial.
Self-pity.
Self-pain.
Phobia.
Apathy.
Darkness.
Depression.
Suicide.
Condolences.

21. Smile of the Satan

Hands of destiny strangle the soul,
Boundless, brutal and blood-laden,
Jubilant in the agony of the whole,
The evil engulfs mortals with abandon.

Heedless to the cries of the crushed,
Casting deathly shadows,
Of sunken past and sore present,
The dreaded dances on dark hallows.

Submerged in a surfeit of pain and gore,
Seething in hideous ire,
The Satan spawns an eerie torrent
Of grief and suffering never felt before.

Anguish in every bone and breath,
Hurt and horror all around,
I hold the fragments of my bleeding heart,
While the hound plays his final part.

22. Summer

Cloudy white mango blooms rustling
in the breeze, unsure of their imminent
destinies; red finicky ants parading
up the bark, bound by invisible decrees;
The giant ball of fire, blinding, scorching the
plumes
of crows relishing pickled rice *vadaams*
on terraces stretched wide like
speckled stars in the Milky Way.

Sturdy straw men s w a y i n g in fields
of yellowing grass, scaring feathered fauna,
their beaks pecking on cracked crevices
of land, like parched roots permeating
the earth; little urchins on banyan
vines *oscillating* like pendulums
in clocks of an antique era, heedless
of the merciless sun or the pleadings
of frenzied mothers.

Long, winding journeys to native lands
past equatorial lines, in sleeper coaches
of bluish serpentine trains, stocked
with scents of the middle class,
heavy baggage in their hearts,

under their seats, hawk-like eyes,
guarding prized possessions, all
day and night, gently rocked by
rails of steel.

23. Morning Moods

My eyelids part languidly
as the morning light pours in;
I lay frozen under the sheets,
hesitant to step away from
the shelter of my dreams.
Acapella of the tweeting birds
is my morning prayer, my hope
for a better day.

But it is never a new day for
the fragments of yesterday and
the day before and the day before
and every other day in the past are
stuck in alleys of the mind, trapped
like insects in silken webs, remnants
of dinner between the gums, a moon
that lingers long after dawn.

My heart silently slips into the realm
of similes, metaphors, and apostrophes;
The reality of lentils, breads, sugars and
spices knocks — ripples in my reverie;
meals to make, lunch boxes to fill, clothes
to press, cries to console, mouths to feed;
spinning stoically in a hurricane through

a morning so morose. Sigh!

Morning chores, inevitable evils
of everyday existence; I gulp down
and rush through the mundane, like
a humanoid, metallic, and lifeless.
Plodding through traffic, insane — I clamber
to the sanctum sanctorum of my workplace,
the holy abode where my mind and body reside
until the earth rolls over to the other side.

24. Phoenix

The darkness of the chapel,
Gods inside,
candles by their side,
casting shadows, imposing and divine.

Statues of stone
lifeless ever,
looming larger,
stare into my soul, restless and rogue.

A tender gaze,
a touch of fondness,
a taste of love, fleeting
I wish for, hands folded, at the holy altar.

Strangers creep in;
They glide away;
Venomous serpents,
shedding skins and shifting shapes.

Words of solace
from friends around;
Allies, never to stay;
Passing clouds in the sky, boundless and blue.

No glittering god,
nor whispering angels
heed my laments
as I bleed on the pristine floors of the Abbey.

Helpless days,
hapless nights in the
ruthless grip of fate,
I weather torrents and torments, infinite.

Roots so rigid,
wings so brave,
I grow in my heart deep
like the simmer of a sleeping volcano.

A lone day this year,
I fight my inner fear
and rise from the ashes upward
breaking the bonds of destiny, like a phoenix
bird.

25. Gulmohar

A lazy Sunday morning;
As the sun beams down,
and the bees hum a tune,
my window gleams, eyes wide open;
I sit by, caffeine in hand, drinking in
the sights and sounds of the world.

The *Gulmohar* greets me with
a gentle nod and a sway, a hushed
'Good morn' I hear. Lovely leaves and
pretty flowers abound, and tiny birds
perched in poise on branches brilliant,
flamboyantly flapping their wings — in unison.

People tread the tarred road below, gleefully
walking past the *Gulmohar*, puny dogs, and their
parents saunter, bonded by leashes and love;
Swanky cars and boisterous bikes whizz
ahead, roaring like a lion unleashed
from a cage — in perennial motion.

Am I the only still life on this canvas?

Dried leaves line the pavement, delicate

reminders of a life once lived, bright and
cherubic in the laps of the *Gulmohar*; I add
commas and semicolons to the free-flowing
verses of my life, to pause and dream, delaying
my fall onto the footpaths of the future.

An array of ants climbs the *Gulmohar*,
mouths laden with food, eyes glowing
with pride, not stopping for applause. A steady
rumble in my stomach! A sprightly squirrel
scurries down to fetch its daily bread as I browse
the breakfast options on the *Swiggy* app.

9 789363 307285